Alex Rodriguez

Alex Rodriguez

Michael Bradley

BENCHMARK BOOKS

MARSHALL CAVENDISH
NEW YORK

Benchmark Books
Marshall Cavendish
99 White Plains Road
Tarrytown, NY 10591-9001
www.marshallcavendish.com

Library of Congress Cataloging-in-Publication Data

Bradley, Michael, 1962-
Alex Rodriguez / by Michael Bradley.
p. cm.—(Benchmark all-stars)
Summary: A biography of "A-Rod," Alex Rodriguez, shortstop for the Texas Rangers,
who is an exceptional player for his age.
Includes bibliographical references (p.   ) and index.
ISBN 0-7614-1757-5 *18.95*
1. Rodriguez, Alex, 1975– Juvenile literature. 2. Baseball players—United States—
Biography—Juvenile literature. [1. Rodriguez, Alex, 1975– 2. Baseball players. 3.
Dominican Americans—Biography.] I. Title II. Series: Bradley, Michael, 1962–
Benchmark all-stars.

GV865.R62B73 2004
796.357'092—dc22

2003022949

Photo Research by Regina Flanagan

Cover: AP/Wide World Photos

Jeff Mitchell/Reuters: 2–3; AP/Wide World Photos: 6, 8, 17, 20, 23, 24, 26, 27, 30, 33,
36, 39, 41; John Cordes/Icon Sports Media: 9; Roy Dabner/AFP/Corbis: 10; Jeff
Christensen/Reuters: 11; Bill Frakes/Sports Illustrated: 12, 15, 16; Damian
Strohmeyer/Sports Illustrated: 18; Al Tielemans/Sports Illustrated: 21; Paul J.
Bereswill/Sports Illustrated: 28; Natalie Fobes/Corbis: 29; Brad Mangin/Sports
Illustrated: 32; Reuters New Media/Corbis: 34; Colin Braley/Reuters: 35; Chuck
Solomon/Sports Illustrated: 38; Reuters: 42.

Series design by Becky Terhune

Printed in Italy

1 3 5 6 4 2

JB
RODRIGUEZ

Contents

Texas Rangers shortstop Alex
Rodriguez shows his stuff!

CHAPTER ONE
The Best Ever

He was the best. Many people thought that. When Ernie Banks played shortstop in the 1950s, 1960s, and early 1970s for the Chicago Cubs, no one else matched him. He hit 512 career homers and slammed more than 2,500 hits. "Mr. Cub" was named to the Hall of Fame.

But as the 2002 season was winding to a close, Banks had some news for the baseball world. He wasn't the best shortstop of all time. It was Alex Rodriguez.

"To me, he is the best," Banks said. "To see this young man play that position with his power and his defensive ability, it's really, really exceptional."

To Banks, "A-Rod" blended the skills of many other great shortstops. He had more power than Cal Ripken Jr., the Baltimore Orioles' legendary performer, and was stronger than Banks. He had better fielding skills than Honus Wagner and Joe Cronin, two stars of baseball's earliest days.

It was hard to argue with Banks—not with the season A-Rod was having. He would finish 2002 by hitting .300, with 57 home runs—a record for shortstops—and a career-high 142 runs batted in (RBIs). It was his fifth consecutive season with more than 40 homers.

And 2003 was even better. At the end of the season, Alex Rodriguez became only the second player from a last place team ever to win baseball's Most Valuable Player Award.

At a time when baseball was filled with great shortstops, like the New York Yankees' Derek Jeter, Nomar Garciaparra of the Boston Red Sox, and the Oakland Athletics' Miguel Tejada, A-Rod had proven himself to be the best.

But February 17, 2004, was the best day. That was the day Alex Rodriguez realized a

Chicago Cubs Hall of Fame star Ernie Banks shares a hug with the man he has called the best shortstop in the business.

lifelong dream to be traded to an East Coast team—the best of the best, the New York Yankees. The Boston Red Sox had tried to grab him, but that trade fell through. Other teams also know how good he is.

"Alex is real, real, real good," said Philadelphia Phillies manager Larry Bowa, himself a former All-Star short-stop. "Alex just keeps getting stronger and stronger. The power he has is just unbelievable. Who knows what he will accomplish before he's done."

It's hard not to talk about the numbers when describing A-Rod. But the biggest figure doesn't have to do with homers or hits. It's about Rodriguez's bank account. Before the 2001 season, he signed a ten-year, $252 million contract to play for Texas. It was easily the biggest deal in the history of all sports, and it was enough to convince him to move from the Seattle Mariners to the Rangers. Texas owner Tom Hicks was betting that Rodriguez's tremendous talent and unlimited *potential* would help make the Rangers contenders every season. "The more I came in contact with the young man, the more I was impressed by him," Hicks said. "The more I knew we had to sign him at whatever cost."

Rodriguez didn't appeal to Hicks just because of his hitting. Or his fielding, which is superb. Or even because, at age twenty-nine, he still has at least ten good years in front of him. Rodriguez's attitude and personality were every bit as important. Hicks was impressed with Rodriguez the man as much as Rodriguez the ballplayer. So are teammates and opponents. It would be easy for Rodriguez to be full of himself. He makes more money than anybody else. He hits homer after homer. He's handsome. Smart. He has a good personality. But it's not in Rodriguez's nature to brag or to treat others poorly.

"Forget about baseball," said Stan Javier, who has been Rodriguez's friend since 1994

Alex Rodriguez stops for a quiet moment before his team loses to the Anaheim Angels, 6-5, on April 16, 2002.

The Texas Ranger knows that, to be the best, he has to train hard. Here, Rodriguez works on his bunting skills during spring training in Surprise, Arizona.

and was a teammate in Seattle. "If my son was that old, Alex is how I'd want him to be, whether he played baseball or not. He's a good man. He's a great guy.

"He's a nice guy. He's a nice guy with an amazing amount of talent, but he's a nice guy, first and foremost."

Rodriguez was raised to treat others with respect. And he was expected to do more than just play baseball. That's why he collects art. Why he has taken college courses in political science and creative writing during the off-season. Why he is fascinated with Leonardo da Vinci, the Italian artist and scientist. And why he gave $1 million to a Miami Boys and

Rodriguez works with Microsoft and HP to donate a computer to a Boys and Girls Club in the United States every time he scores an RBI.

Girls Club to build a new baseball facility and a learning center. "He's Mr. Clean," said former Seattle teammate David Segui. "He's milk-and-cookies. He doesn't like to hear that, but he is. He likes everybody in [the clubhouse] to think he's some kind of thug from Miami, but he's as milk-and-cookies as it gets."

Rodriguez works hard to become better. He takes extra ground balls before games. He'll hit extra if he needs to. Sure, he likes to relax, whether he's listening to Frank Sinatra compact discs or playing with his dogs (a German shepherd named Gypsy and a yellow Labrador called Shorty). But when it's time to work, Rodriguez is ready. That desire makes him a great leader.

"I have incredible *motivation* to go out and improve every day," Rodriguez said. "Integrity-wise, I cannot allow whether the team is winning or not to affect me. I'm going to give maximum effort. I have to look at myself every day and judge myself on my work ethic."

Others are watching, too. And their *verdict* is in: Alex Rodriguez is one of baseball's absolute best.

Alex Rodriguez became a star—or at least developed star potential—under the leadership of coach Rich Hofman at Westminster Christian School in Miami.

CHAPTER TWO

On the Right Path

When Alex was growing up, he had a poster of Orioles shortstop Cal Ripken Jr. in his room. On the back of his uniform was the number 3, in homage to another of his boyhood heroes, Atlanta and Philadelphia All-Star Dale Murphy. Both were great players. Both were also fine role models.

That's how it was for Alex. He didn't root just for the player. He wanted to cheer for the person. It was a lesson he had learned from his mother, Lourdes. Many had taken their natural abilities and become stars. Not so many had been *exemplary* people off the field, too. Any player who wanted to win Alex's loyalties would have to do both. That's why he became a Keith Hernandez fan. When Alex was a boy, he and a friend were hanging around the New York Mets' spring training center one afternoon after practice. Hernandez, the Mets' first baseman, saw them and invited them into the clubhouse, where he gave them autographs and showed them around. From then on, Alex was a Hernandez fan. And when he made the majors, he was sure to sign as many autographs as he could.

"My mom always said, 'I don't care if you turn out to be a terrible ballplayer; I just want you to be a good person,'" Alex said. "That's the most important thing to me. Like Cal or Dale Murphy, I want people to look at me and say, 'He's a good person.'"

> "My mom always said, 'I don't care if you turn out to be a terrible ballplayer; I just want you to be a good person.' That's the most important thing to me."
> —Alex Rodriguez

Alex was born on July 27, 1975, in New York City, to Lourdes and Victor Rodriguez. Victor was a shoe salesman, but he loved baseball. When Alex was four, he moved the family to the Dominican Republic, so that Victor—a catcher—could play baseball professionally there. That was where Alex saw his first baseball games. Four years later, the family moved again, this time to the Miami suburbs.

When Alex was ten, Victor moved out, leaving Lourdes to raise him, his older brother, Joe, and his sister, Susy, by herself. She went to work as a secretary and a waitress to earn the money needed to support the family. Alex grew very close to his mother. When she came home late at night from the restaurant where she worked, Alex would be up. The two would talk while Alex counted the tip money she received. The tight bond that formed between them still exists today. Meanwhile, Susy kept watch over Alex's studies (he dreamed of being a doctor or lawyer while in grade school), and Joe taught him about sports. Lourdes, however, was the main influence.

"I kept thinking my father would come back, but he never did," Alex said. "But it was okay. All the love I had for him I just gave to my mother. She deserved it."

While Lourdes worked hard at two jobs to feed, clothe, and shelter her family, Alex put in long hours on the baseball diamond. At first, he played at a Boys and Girls Club in the Miami area for Eddie Rodriguez (no relation), who became something of a second father to him. In 1986, when Alex was eleven, he was part of a team that won the Pony League Baseball championship, a national competition involving players of little-league age.

That was the first inkling that Alex was a special baseball player. Further evidence came at Westminster Christian School in Miami. Lourdes may not have been rich, but she earned enough to send Alex to that private school, which had about a hundred male students in grades ten through twelve. Under the watchful eye of coach Rich Hofman, another influential figure in Alex's life, Alex became a star. Although he struggled at the plate as a sophomore, hitting just .280, he worked hard to improve. Alex took extra batting practice and did sit-ups and push-ups to get stronger. It all worked.

Professional scouts were aware of Rodriguez's Major League potential when he was only fourteen years old!

Alex Rodriguez tags out an opposing player in a high school game.

Alex was a three-time high school All-American. At age fourteen, professional *scouts* were already saying he might be the top pick in the major-league draft, even though he was three years away from being eligible. "Coaching Alex is a once-in-a-lifetime experience," Hofman said.

Baseball wasn't Alex's only sporting love. He also played quarterback at Westminster and idolized San Francisco 49ers star quarterback Joe Montana. Alex was the *point guard* on the

Westminster basketball team and tried to imitate Magic Johnson, who played that position for the Los Angeles Lakers. But baseball was his game, and he devoted himself to it. He had a big junior year, helping Westminster earn the *USA Today* national championship. The following season, Alex was even better. He hit .505 and had the scouts excited over his potential. Some called him the next Cal Ripken Jr. But despite the great *statistics* and praise, Alex wasn't perfect. He proved that in the Florida state championship game, when his error cost Westminster the title.

Alex Rodriguez is all smiles as the Seattle Mariners ask him to join their baseball team, making him the first overall pick in the 1993 Major League draft.

"It's always in my mind," he said. "That's why I don't take anything for granted."

Midway through his senior year, Alex announced that he was going to play baseball at the University of Miami. But the Seattle Mariners changed those plans in June 1993, when they made Alex the first overall pick in the Major League draft. It took most of the summer for them to work out a contract, but the deal was done. Alex wasn't going to college. He was heading for the world of professional baseball with the hope of becoming a great player.

And a great person.

Alex Rodriguez in action on the
Seattle field.

CHAPTER THREE
Making the Big Leagues

It went down to the final hours. Rodriguez had been drafted by the Seattle Mariners, but he didn't seem too anxious to make the 3,000-mile trip from Miami to the Pacific Northwest. The idea of moving that far from home, from Lourdes and Joe and Susy, wasn't all that attractive. He could stay home and attend the University of Miami, and everything would be fine.

Things didn't move that quickly with Seattle in the summer of 1993. Alex's agent, Scott Boras, wouldn't allow the Mariners' *representatives* to meet in person with the Rodriguez family. Offers and counteroffers were made by fax machine. It was a long, drawn-out, frustrating process that left both sides unhappy. It looked like Rodriguez wouldn't make it to Seattle.

Then came the breakthrough. Just hours before he was to begin university classes at Miami—a move that would make him ineligible for professional play for the next three years, according to Major League baseball's rules—Rodriguez signed a contract. He didn't really want to go to the university. He was using it as a threat. He wanted to scare the Mariners into giving him more money in a contract by saying that they could lose him. Seattle didn't lose him. The sides agreed on a contract for three years and $1.3 million. Rodriguez was a Mariner. He celebrated by buying a Jeep Cherokee. And by going to the minor leagues.

Young fans wait their turn for autographs from the newly drafted Seattle Mariner.

The month of September was a whirlwind for Rodriguez. He played at every level of the Seattle organization, beginning at Class A, the lowest, and moving all the way up to the majors. He lasted just seventeen games with the Mariners but was too young and inexperienced to stick around with the big club. Rodriguez's numbers with Seattle weren't that impressive. He hit just .204, had no homers, and struck out 20 times in 57 trips to the plate. He may have been the number one pick, but he wasn't a star—yet. Rodriguez was eventually sent back to Calgary, where the Mariners' AAA team played. (AAA is the level just below the majors.) Even though he hadn't stayed up in the majors, ending his first professional season at the highest level of minor-league baseball was a significant accomplishment.

Things became tougher that winter. Rodriguez played ball in the Dominican Republic, hoping to hone his skills and be ready to start in Seattle in 1995. The experience was difficult on many levels. First, Rodriguez had to deal with memories of returning to the place where he had lived for three years as a small child. He also had to deal with the rough-edged nature of the Dominican game, which was played on fields that were filled with rocks and had poorly tended grass, in front of often-unforgiving crowds. He hit just .179 in three months of play and struggled to field well.

Back in the big leagues, Seattle Mariner Alex Rodriguez makes a throw in a game against the Baltimore Orioles on June 8, 1995.

"It was the toughest experience of my life," he said. "I got my tail kicked and learned how hard the game can be. It was brutal, but I recommend it to every young player."

Thus hardened, Rodriguez went to spring training in 1995 expecting to grab the starting shortstop position and spend the season in Seattle. It didn't happen. Luis Sojo got the job, and Alex was sent to Tacoma, the Mariners' new Class AAA team. Although he would yo-yo between the minors and the big club, being called up three times, Alex

Baseball Terms

Like all other sports, baseball has a language of its own. Here are some popular terms and their definitions.

Minor leagues: The levels of baseball below the big leagues. Each team has a collection of minor-league teams at several levels, beginning with the lowest (rookie) and moving up to Class A, Class AA, and Class AAA.

Pinch hitter: A player who gets to hit in place of a teammate who is scheduled to bat. Pinch hitters are often used in place of pitchers, who are usually not good hitters.

Runs batted in (RBIs): This is a statistic that measures how many runners a hitter brings home when he is at bat. If a runner scores because a teammate gets a hit, a walk, or even makes a fly-out, the hitter earns an RBI. If someone has 100 RBIs in a season, he is considered a very successful hitter.

Sent down: This occurs when a player who has been in the big leagues must go back and play in the minors to get some more experience or improve his play.

Shortstop: The position in the infield between second and third bases. The shortstop is known for excellent fielding, but many current players in that position are strong hitters, too.

Wild card: A team that makes the playoffs even though it has not won any of the American and National leagues' six divisions. The wild cards are the teams in each league with the best record of all the non-division winners.

played only forty-eight games in the majors, hitting just .232 in 142 at-bats.

But it was still a great experience for Rodriguez. He was called up for good on August 31 and played a supporting role in the Mariners' great comeback that captured the American League West Division title. He also got a great view of Seattle's thrilling first-round playoff upset of the Yankees. Granted, that *perspective* was from the Mariners' bench, but Rodriguez didn't mind. He was learning and growing.

"It was an awesome experience," he said. "I was twenty years old. It would have been *ludicrous* for me to think I should have been in there. I understood my role—I was there to pinch-run or fill in if someone got hurt— and it didn't bother me at all."

Rodriguez wasn't just a cheerleader. He spent plenty of time working before and after games. And from the bench, he absorbed as much as he could. He studied the players. Watched pitchers. Learned how his veteran teammates prepared for games.

"I think he learned a lot just being around down the stretch," said then-Seattle manager Lou Piniella. "Even though we all knew he was our shortstop of the future, it wouldn't have been fair to the guys on the field or to Alex [to put him in the starting lineup]."

So, Rodriguez learned and listened. And he impressed his new teammates

> "It was an awesome experience. I was twenty years old. It would have been ludicrous for me to think I should have been in there. I understood my role—I was there to pinch-run or fill in if someone got hurt—and it didn't bother me at all."
>
> —Alex Rodriguez

with his dedication. He could have been angry at being a substitute. After all, he was the top pick in the 1993 draft and had signed a big contract. Instead, he was humble. He wanted to grow as a player. And no one could question his dedication.

"He had that from the beginning," said Edgar Martinez, Seattle's designated hitter in 1995, and one of the game's most respected players. "As a young player, he worked really hard all the time."

All of that effort was about to pay off—in a big way.

Part of Rodriguez's appeal is how much he cares for others. Here, he comforts teammate Joey Cora after the team lost to the Cleveland Indians, 4-0. With that game, the Indians won the American League championship for 1995.

Seattle Mariners Alex Rodriguez makes a double-play against the New York Yankees on May 26, 1996. The Mariners went on to win, 4-3.

CHAPTER FOUR

Hitting It Big

After spending 1995 as a backup and struggling to find time in the Mariners' lineup, Rodriguez wondered what the 1996 campaign would hold. As it turns out, it held a lot. A whole lot.

Instead of struggling, as he had during his first two seasons as a professional, Rodriguez put together one of the greatest seasons ever by a shortstop. Not only did he hit with great power and for a high average, but he also fielded like a ten-year veteran. Rodriguez's birth certificate may have said he turned twenty-one in 1996, but he was playing like someone much older and more experienced. And there was no shortage of praise for baseball's newest sensation.

"Alex Rodriguez is going to do things I never came close to doing," former Chicago Cubs Hall of Fame shortstop Ernie Banks said. "I don't want to put pressure on him, but he's going to set a new standard for shortstops."

"Let's be honest," said Alan Trammell, a former star shortstop for Detroit. "The year he had could be the best year a shortstop has ever had."

Rodriguez's numbers were outrageous. He led the American League with a .358 batting

["Alex Rodriguez is going to do things I never came close to doing. I don't want to put pressure on him, but he's going to set a new standard for shortstops."
—Ernie Banks

average, the first shortstop to do so since the Cleveland Indians' Lou Boudreau did it in 1944. He hit 36 home runs, knocked in 123 runs, and scored a league-leading 141 times. He led the league with 54 doubles and was second with 215 hits. Rodriguez made only 15 errors in 657 fielding chances and was the youngest shortstop ever to play in the All-Star game. About the only disappointment Rodriguez encountered came when the Most Valuable Player (MVP) ballots were counted. He finished second, by three votes, to Texas's Juan Gonzalez. It was a magnificent year, a year that earned him praise from one of his heroes.

His first grand slam! It happened in the second inning playing against the Detroit Tigers on Thursday, April 18, 1996.

"All that Alex seems to need is experience to become the shortstop everyone else will be watching in our league," Cal Ripken Jr. said. "I'm still having a good time out there, just playing. But the future belongs to Alex Rodriguez."

Not everything was perfect during the 1996 season. Seattle won eighty-five games but finished second to Texas in the American League West standings. That meant no post-season play. Also, there was some concern among the veteran Mariners that Rodriguez's big season would create unfair expectations. Here he was, only twenty-one years old, and already people were comparing him with the game's best short-stops. That was great to hear, but it was also dangerous talk. Nobody could keep up that pace, could they?

"I just hope people don't expect him to put up those numbers every year," said Seattle outfielder Ken Griffey Jr., himself a star performer. "I hope that they're not going to say he had a bad year, if he hits .330, with 25 homers, and 90 RBIs. I don't want him feeling he has to do this every year."

Rodriguez wasn't intimidated by the expectations. Or the pressure. He was having

Seattle Mariners shortstop Rodriguez takes a flying leap into the air as he forces Toronto Blue Jays Joe Carter out at second during the first inning of a game on April 27, 1997.

fun and was grateful for the opportunity to shine. "I really feel I've been given this gift, that I've been blessed," he said. "I thank the Lord for that, but I have to remember that it can be taken away, too."

Nobody took Rodriguez's gifts away in 1997, but his numbers did drop some. He still had a great season, but it looked a little light compared to 1996. Rodriguez hit .300, slugged 23 homers, and knocked in 84 runs. He scored 100 times, hit 40 doubles, and stole

Alex Rodriguez cuts a dashing figure as he fields a game against the New York Yankees.

29 bases. His fielding was still strong, but he made 24 errors, which would turn out to be a career high. Most players would have been thrilled with that season, especially since the Mariners won the West with a franchise-record ninety victories. For Rodriguez, however, it was a small step backward.

It was nothing he couldn't handle. As 1998 dawned, Rodriguez still had big goals. He was gunning to become a member of the exclusive 40-homer, 40-stolen bases club. Only San Francisco Giants' Barry Bonds, and José Canseco, then of the Oakland A's, had ever accomplished that. Rodriguez went after the record with his trademark blend of determination and preparation. He hired a personal trainer after the 1997 campaign and worked with him five or six times a week. When the A's came to Seattle during the season, he sought out Oakland outfielder Rickey Henderson, the game's greatest-ever base stealer, and asked question after question about how best to run the bases.

It all paid off. Rodriguez stole 46 bases and hit 42 homers to become, at twenty-three years old, the youngest player to accomplish the 40-40 double. His numbers were up across the board. He hit .310, knocked in 124 runs, scored 123 times, had 213 hits, and a career-best 5 triples. He upped his fielding chances by more than 100 (from 627 to 731) and dropped his errors to 18. The Mariners finished $11\text{-}1/_2$ games back in the standings, but Rodriguez couldn't hang his head. His 40-40 achievement was quite an accomplishment.

"It's just a great lesson for me as a young player about the necessity of hard work," Rodriguez said. "That's what I attribute my success to [in 1998], all my work. It's probably the thing I'm most proud of, more than being batting champion [in 1996]. This is something I'm very, very proud of and something I'll never forget."

There would be other great moments to come, but the next two seasons would be very trying for Rodriguez. A decision was looming, and it wouldn't be an easy one.

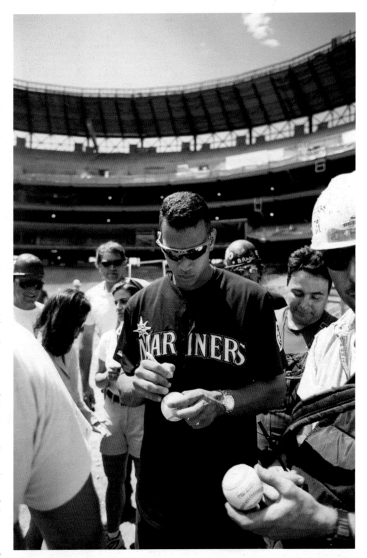

Construction workers wait for autographed basballs from Alex Rodriguez at a topping-out ceremony at Safeco Field in Seattle.

Seattle Mariners Alex Rodriguez reaches out for a high five after scoring the winning run in the tenth inning against the Oakland Athletics in Seattle on July 22, 1999.

CHAPTER FIVE

Decisions, Decisions

The 1998 season had been fabulous for Rodriguez. He had survived his "sophomore slump" of 1997—even though it wasn't much of a slump—and was back among the game's best. He entered the 1999 campaign energized and excited to be moving with the Mariners from the sterile confines of the Kingdome into brand new Safeco Field, an open-air ballpark that was truly state-of-the-art.

But there was trouble on the horizon. First, Rodriguez spent the month of April and the beginning of May on the disabled list with a knee injury. That pretty much guaranteed he wouldn't duplicate the previous season's 40-40 performance. More worrisome, however, was talk about the futures of Rodriguez and Ken Griffey Jr. in Seattle. Griffey's contract was due to end after the 1999 season, while Rodriguez was to be a free agent after 2000. There were rumors that one or both could be traded. Many wondered whether either would return to the Mariners when it was time to sign a new contract, or whether the club could afford to pay them. Although the answers to most questions for Rodriguez were still more than a full year away, he was still pestered by reporters.

"I can't control it anyway, so why should I worry about it," Rodriguez said about trade rumors and his future with the Mariners. "As I told the Seattle media, I love playing in Seattle. [Ken]

Griffey's dad told him your first major league team is always special. I feel the same way.

"But the bottom line is what direction this team wants to go. Does management want to hang around in the middle of the pack or make the moves necessary to win a championship?"

Judging by Seattle's finish in 1999, Rodriguez had every right to question the team's direction. Despite boasting two of the game's top players—Rodriguez and Griffey—Seattle slumped to third in the American League West standings, with a disappointing 79-83 record. It marked the second straight year Seattle had missed the playoffs. "Those were two of the toughest seasons of my career," Rodriguez would say three years later. Not that Rodriguez's numbers were below-*par*. Although his batting average slipped to .285, he smacked 42 homers, drove in 111 runs, and scored 110 times. He stole 21 bases and made just 14 errors. With each game, Rodriguez was establishing himself further as one of baseball's best.

"He's a complete player," said Rudy Terrasas, a scout for the Texas Rangers. "He can beat you in all facets of the game—with his power, his speed, and his glove. And he's still young, with a tremendous *upside*. People who play like he does are usually 28, 29, 30 years old. He's not even 24 and doing it. For my money, if I was starting a club and needed a shortstop . . . he'd be my choice."

Alex Rodriguez is tagged out as he slides into home plate in action against the Cleveland Indians on August 12, 2000.

The 1999 season was difficult because of the Mariners' finish, but 2000 brought its own set of troubles. Griffey was gone, traded during the off-season to Cincinnati. Although they weren't the closest of friends, they had developed a deep mutual respect. Now, it was Rodriguez's team, and many wanted to know how he would lead it. More importantly, they wanted to know if he would even be with the club in 2001. Rodriguez was polite when questioned but wasn't about to reveal his plans. "I've had to deal with a lot more adversity than this," he said. "This is not a problem. This is a win-win situation. Whatever happens, I'm prepared."

Rodriguez was ready on the field, too. Despite the loss of Griffey, the Mariners earned a wild-card berth to the playoffs, thanks to having the best record of the teams that didn't win a division. Seattle then dumped the Chicago White Sox in the first round of the playoffs and held its own against the eventual World Series champion New York Yankees, falling in the post-season's second round in six games.

Number 3 led the way. Rodriguez hit .316, slammed 41 homers, knocked in a career-best 132 RBIs, and earned 34 doubles. He scored 134 runs, drew 100 walks, and committed just 10 errors. It

Rodriguez leaps over New York Yankees' Derek Jeter during a double play in the first inning of Game Three of the American League Championship Series on October 13, 2000.

was a superstar performance and a great way for Alex to say goodbye to the Mariners' fans, if that was indeed his plan. "I absolutely see *scenarios* where I'm in Seattle next year," Rodriguez said during the season. "But at the same time, I see scenarios where I'm elsewhere."

Once the free-agent merry-go-round started to turn, it was obvious that Rodriguez would be elsewhere. And soon, it was revealed that the "elsewhere" would be Texas. Rangers owner Tom Hicks, *flush* with cash after signing a big deal to televise Texas games locally, made a strong run at Rodriguez. So strong, in fact, that he blew away every other offer. When Rodriguez finally signed on the dotted line, the sports world was stunned. Ten years, $252 million. It was easily the largest contract signed in sports history.

Many criticized Rodriguez for taking the

A winner from the start, Alex Rodriguez smiles happily as he announces his ten-year, $252 million deal with the Texas Rangers, the world's biggest single player sports contract.

A History of the Texas Rangers

The Texas Rangers franchise began its existence in, of all places, Washington, D.C. After the 1960 season, the American League moved the existing Washington Senators club to Minnesota, where they became the Twins. A "new" Senators team was placed in D.C., where it remained for eleven years. It wasn't exactly a memorable stay. The Senators had just one winning season (1969) before moving to Arlington, a suburb of Dallas, to become the Rangers.

In Texas, the team was more successful than its predecessor, but it took some time. The Rangers finally won the franchise's first division title in 1994. They didn't exactly tear up the league, finishing with a 52-62 record. There was no post-season that year, because the players were on strike for a bigger share of the money made by team owners. That shortened the season by forty-nine games.

Things improved in the late 1990s. Texas won the West in 1996, 1998, and 1999. But each time, they lost in the first round of the playoffs to the New York Yankees, winning just one game in the process.

S–t–r–e–t–c–h! No matter how much he earns, Alex Rodriguez works harder than anyone to keep in shape for the season. Here, a trainer works on him during his first day of training camp as a Texas Ranger.

money—as if they wouldn't have jumped at such a pile of cash themselves. He had said he wanted to play for a team that was committed to winning, and here was Texas, which had lost 91 games in 2000 and had won just one playoff contest in its entire forty-year history. But Rodriguez believed that he could help turn things around. He liked Hicks. He wanted to be part of something big.

"People criticized me for coming to Texas," Rodriguez said. "I didn't sign for one year. I saw what happened in Seattle when we were close [to winning it all], and management didn't get the big player that can put you over the top. I'm convinced Mr. Hicks will do what it takes to win. There is nothing I would like to do more than to prove him right about my contract."

Rodriguez would get that chance—under intense scrutiny.

Texas Ranger Alex Rodriguez limbers up for batting practice during spring training.

CHAPTER SIX

Deep in the Heart of Texas

It wasn't the best way to convince people that you were worth $252 million. Rodriguez was ready to live under the microscope in Texas, but his regular-season debut for the Rangers didn't inspire much confidence. All of a sudden, Rodriguez wasn't the power-hitting, smooth-fielding star who would lead the Rangers to great things. He looked like a clumsy rookie.

On his first official chance at shortstop for Texas, Rodriguez committed an error. It was the 2001 opener against Toronto in San Juan, Puerto Rico, as part of Major League baseball's effort to promote the game on the island. He fielded a grounder cleanly but threw the ball wildly past first base. The next time he got the ball, Rodriguez slipped and fell down while trying to turn a double play. And to finish off a crazy afternoon, Alex fell on his face while trying to field a ground ball. Rodriguez did hit a pair of singles and scored the Rangers' lone run in an 8-1 loss, but it wasn't the greatest debut.

"You have to start somewhere," Rodriguez said after the game. "[The first game] had a little of everything—error, slip, hit . . . You just move on."

Rodriguez's off-season had been filled with tremendous interest—and some conflict— over his new contract. He was no longer just Alex Rodriguez, shortstop. Now, he was The Amazing $252 Million Man. Some reporters and broadcasters criticized him for being

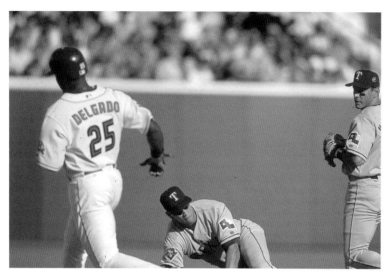

Oops! Rodriguez fields and slips while trying to turn a double play against the Toronto Blue Jays.

greedy. Even some owners of other teams were upset, because his big contract meant that other players would want huge amounts of money, at a time when many clubs were having economic troubles. But Rodriguez didn't worry too much about the *analysis*, even when it was negative. And he didn't listen too closely when people praised him. Despite his newfound wealth, he was still Rodriguez, trying to be a good person, first and foremost.

"If I told you that [praise] made me feel good, then every time somebody tells me I'm not worth it, it should bother me, right?" he asked. "You can't have it both ways, so I don't take any of it to heart. This is the first time I've been singled out like this. It's as though I'm walking around with a sign around my neck that says '252.' How will I react? I've never been in this position, so I can't tell you for sure. I think I'll be fine."

Rodriguez's start in Texas may have been shaky, but his first full season was solid. He hit .318, pounded a career-high 52 homers—a single-season record for shortstops—knocked in 135 runs, and scored 133 times. He had 201 hits, 34 doubles, and 75 walks. It was a tremendous season, especially since many people were rooting for him to fail because of his huge contract.

But the Rangers couldn't boast the same success. The team finished with a disappointing 73-89 record, in last place in the American League West Division. Even though Rodriguez had been everything Texas fans had hoped he would be, the rest of the team had huge holes. The pitching staff was thin. The team's defense was weak. And there wasn't enough pop in the batting order to support Rodriguez's efforts. Rodriguez was a great player, but baseball is a team sport.

The media would grab onto that fact in 2002 with a *vengeance*. Despite playing much of the year on a bad ankle, Rodriguez had a tremendous season. He entered September with a strong chance at becoming just the fifth man to hit 60 homers. (The other four were Babe Ruth, Roger Maris, Mark McGwire, and Sammy Sosa.) He was knocking in runs at a pace of nearly one per game. He was fielding as well as he had ever fielded (just 10 errors in a career-high 741 chances). He was

> **"It's as though I'm walking around with a sign around my neck that says '252.' How will I react? I've never been in this position, so I can't tell you for sure. I think I'll be fine."**
> **—Alex Rodriguez**

leading in the clubhouse by encouraging teammates. He was having a year worthy of the Most Valuable Player award. But there was one problem: Texas was in last place. Again. The Rangers had been there all year and would finish the season there, courtesy of a 72-90 record. They were virtually eliminated from post-season consideration by the time Rodriguez turned twenty-seven, in July. As Alex continued to put up great numbers, the debate began. Did he deserve the award? Since only four MVPs in baseball history had come from teams with losing records, the odds weren't in Rodriguez's favor. Some thought Oakland A's shortstop Miguel Tejada deserved it. Others were in favor of New York Yankees second baseman Alfonso Soriano. Rodriguez was having a great season, but Texas was in last place. Many acknowledged Rodriguez's greatness but said the MVP didn't go to the best player, rather the one who

His first season didn't start so well, but Rodriguez took it in stride. Here he is charged with a throwing error against Detroit Tigers Deivi Cruz on May 10, 2001.

meant the most to a winning team.

"I would give it to Tejada," said Toronto Blue Jays general manager J. P. Ricciardi. "Do I think Tejada is a better player? No. A-Rod is the best in the league, and he might be the best ever before it's all said and done. But without Tejada, I don't think the A's are in [playoff] contention."

"You can't be that valuable when you're on a last-place club," then-Tampa Bay Devil Rays manager Hal McRae said.

In 1996 when he had his huge breakout season, Rodriguez said he didn't deserve the MVP award. This time, he wasn't so humble. He realized that once you receive the MVP, it stays with you your whole career. For that one year, you were the best.

"Sure, I'd be disappointed if I'm not the MVP," he said. "I've been in the race a few times. I've come close.

"I deserve it."

In the end, Rodriguez didn't win the award. It went to Tejada. But that couldn't take away from his great season. And those around baseball understood how talented he was. "He's the best player I've ever seen," Toronto manager Carlos Tosca said.

The scary thing was, he was going to get better. With more than ten years ahead of him, there was no limit to what Alex Rodriguez could do and become.

Rodriguez was primed for having an even better season in 2003. He wanted more than just great individual numbers.

⭐ Choosing the Most Valuable Player

The Most Valuable Player award is one of baseball's most *prestigious*. It goes to the player in each league, American and National, who has the greatest effect on his team. Without him, would the club be as successful? That's the big question.

The payoff is big, too. The MVP is the type of honor that can help a player when he is considered for the Hall of Fame after his career ends. And it can help tremendously in future contract negotiations.

Here's how the awards are chosen. Two baseball writers from each team-city can vote on the MVP of the respective league. The voters are chosen by the Baseball Writers' Association, to which most newspaper and magazine writers belong. Each voter ranks his candidates from 1-through-10. Each ranking carries a certain point value. A first-place ranking means fourteen points. Second place is nine. Third is eight, and so on, down to tenth place. When all the votes are counted and points assigned, the player with the most points wins.

Rodriguez wanted to win. It didn't happen. Texas once again finished last in the American League West. The Rangers' 71-91 record left them twenty-five games behind division winner Oakland in the standings. The poor season came courtesy of the same old culprits: weak pitching and not enough lineup strength around Rodriguez. Although some new talent, most notably Hank Blalock and Mark Teixara, gave hope for the future, the present was again disappointing.

Rodriguez didn't match the previous year's bonanza, but few could be upset with his performance. He hit .298, with 47 homers, and 118 RBIs. Most believed he was the best player in baseball, and that made Rodriguez happy. He proved it in 2003 by winning the Most Valuable Player award.

And in 2004, Alex Rodriguez traded his Texas Rangers jersey for the New York Yankees' white and blue, going from shortstop to third baseman. That didn't bother him at all.

Longtime friends and now teammates—new third baseman Alex Rodriguez (l) and New York Yankees captain and shortstop Derek Jeter answer questions at the press conference called to announce that Rodriguez had joined the team.

"To me, it was a very easy decision. To me, this came down to winning," Rodriguez said at the February 17, 2004, press conference at which his trade to the Yankees was announced.

And no wonder. Winning and being the best is what Rodriguez is all about—in whatever position he is assigned.

stats

Stats

Alex Rodriguez

Born:	July 27, 1975
Birthplace:	New York, New York
High School:	Westminster Christian School
Height:	6' 3" (191 cm)
Weight:	210 lbs. (95 kg)
Team:	Texas Rangers
Position:	SS (shortstop)

SEASON	GM	AB	R	H	2B	3B	HR	RBIs	SB	AVG
1994	17	54	4	11	0	0	0	2	3	.204
1995	48	142	15	33	6	2	5	19	4	.232
1996	146	601	141	215	54	1	36	123	15	.358
1997	141	587	100	176	40	3	23	84	29	.300
1998	161	686	123	213	35	5	42	124	46	.310
1999	129	502	110	143	25	0	42	111	21	.285
2000	148	554	134	175	34	2	41	132	15	.316
2001	162	632	133	201	34	1	52	135	18	.318
2002	162	624	125	187	27	2	57	142	9	.300
2003	161	607	124	181	30	6	47	118	17	.298
Career	1275	4989	1009	1535	285	22	345	990	177	.308

Source:www.mlb.com

GLOSSARY

analysis—The breaking down of something that happens into smaller parts to try to understand why it happened. The analysis of someone's success would include finding the reasons behind the achievement.

exemplary—So good—usually in behavior—as to serve as a model for others.

flush—Filled with success or money. A person is flush if he or she has just received a large payment or has achieved something great and is enjoying that success.

ludicrous—Silly, or ridiculous.

motivation—A person's reason for performing at a high level. Some people are motivated by money. Others want to prove critics wrong. Still more are simply motivated to be the absolute best they can be.

par—An established value of something or someone's performance. If a person or thing exceeds that level, it is known as above par. A lesser outcome would be below par.

perspective—A person's view of a situation. Even though something may happen a certain way, many people may look at it differently and have a different outlook on how it happened and what it means.

point guard—The position on a basketball team that involves much ball-handling, passing, and the ability to get teammates to do what the coach wants them to do.

potential—What something or someone can become over time. A player with great potential could be a star, provided he or she works hard, stays clear of injury, and gets the chance to perform.

prestigious—A person or event with great influence because of success or wealth.

representatives—People who work on behalf of someone else. A representative will do his or her best to make sure that person's interests are given top consideration.

scenarios—Various possible outcomes of a situation. If someone is considering what might happen, he or she will think of various scenarios and try to prepare for them.

scouts—Baseball experts whose job it is to find talented players and determine whether they are good enough to be signed to contracts with a specific team.

statistics—Numeric measurements of a person's talent in a given field. In baseball, players are rated according to how many home runs they hit, what their batting average is, or how many runs they drive in. Pitchers are measured by wins versus losses and strikeouts, among others.

upside—The possible good things that a person or thing may deliver. A player with a large upside is thought to have the chance to be a star.

vengeance—The desire to respond to someone's negative actions or criticism with a strong action. Players often play with a vengeance if they believe someone has criticized them falsely, and they want to prove that person wrong.

verdict—A decision reached in some form of dispute. Court verdicts determine whether someone is guilty or innocent. Other verdicts name winners of contests or votes.

Find Out More

Books

Christopher, Matt. *On The Field. Alex Rodriguez*. New York: Little Brown & Co., 2002.

Covert, Kim. *Alex Rodriguez*. Mankato, MN: Capstone Press, 2002.

Macnow, Glen. *Sports Great Alex Rodriguez*. Berkeley Heights, NJ: Enslow Publishers, 2002.

Stewart, Mark. *Alex Rodriguez: Gunning for Greatness*. Brookfield, CT: Millbrook Press Trade, 1999.

Web Sites

ESPN Site
http://www.ESPN.go.com/mlb/players/profile?statsld=5275

Major League Baseball Site
http://www.MLB.com/NASApp/mlb/tex/team/tex_player_bio.jsp?frame=mlb&playerid=121347